Strength Beneath the Scars

A series of *poems* tell the story.

Bridget Ford

Soul. Truth. Love. Poetry. LC

Copyright © 2021 Bridget Ford

All rights reserved. No part of this book may be reproduced or used in any manner without the prior written permission of the copyright owner, except for the use of brief quotations in a book review.

ISBN: 978-1-7379689-0-0 (Paperback)
ISBN: 978-1-7379689-2-4 (Hardback)

First paperback edition November 2021.

Cover art by Pixabay.

Soul. Truth. Love. Poetry. LC
poemstellthestory@gmail.com
poemstellthestory.com

To those still searching for peace.

Table of Contents

Thank you	6
Acknowledgements	7
Introduction	8

Chapter 1: Prisoner

	1.	Prisoner	10
	2.	Suicide	11
	3.	Code Blue	12
	4.	Tired	13
	5.	Trapped	14
	6.	Private Battle	15
	7.	Reported by a Blind Eye	16
	8.	Transparency	17
	9.	Broken Trust	18
	10.	Decrepit Love	19

Chapter 2: Emptiness — 21

	1.	Abandoned	22
	2.	As a Mother	23
	3.	Motherly Love	24
	4.	On my Own	25
	5.	Forced Independence	26
	6.	Concealed Sadness	27
	7.	Butchered Love	28
	8.	Superwoman	29

Chapter 3: Hope — 30

	1.	Hope	31
	2.	Blurred Happiness	32
	3.	Last Through the Seasons	33
	4.	Left in the Night	34
	5.	Royalty Just the Same	35
	6.	Seasoned Wisdom	36
	7.	Innocent Dreams	37
	8.	I Deserve It	38
	9.	The Beauty of a Man	39

Chapter 4: Chasing Peace   41
1. Strength of a Woman   42
2. Light in Darkness   43
3. Cries Never Heard   44
4. Silent & Deadly   45
5. Fool's Gold   46
6. Only Time Will Tell   47
7. Memories   48
8. Hidden Desires   49
9. One Wish   50
10. The Rock Behind the Glass   51
11. Growth   52
12. Just Be Still   53
13. A Song's Embrace   54
14. Friendship   55
15. Love   56
16. Comprehension of Peace   57

Chapter 5: Self-Made   59
1. Here I Stand   60
2. Who Comforts Me?   61
3. Journey to Peace   62
4. Beauty from Within   63
5. Written Therapy   64
6. Assured Peace   65
7. Be Present   66
8. It's Only a Test   67
9. My Purpose   68
10. Justified Peace   69
11. Unstoppable   70

About the Author   72
Craving More?   74
Letter to You   75

To those who found a place for me in their heart.

Thank You

*Thank you for your ear,
Thank you for your love,
Thank you for your peace that came from God above.
I never had to question where I rest in your heart.
It's your kind words and generosity that almost made me fall apart.
The tears I cry now, don't all burn my flesh.
The love I feel now, isn't like a game of chess.
It's your love and your spirit that brought me closer to the moon.
Your love and generosity that changed my attitude.
True love I can see, you made me believe,
I can really have people who truly love me.*

Bridget Ford

Acknowledgments

Special thanks to my husband, Nivek Ford, for listening to my poems after the sky turned gray. Thank you for occupying our child as I made my heart visible to the eyes of those unsure of the thoughts that flooded my mind. Thank you so much for all you do. Love you.

Sweet thanks to my baby boy, Isaiah, for being my support system by giving me a reason to wake up in the morning and complete the dream I started so long ago. Mommy loves you. You mean more to me than you could ever imagine.

I was 16 years old when I found the comfort in writing. Poems became my relief, my peace, and my person. Trey, you began listening to my poems at 17. You made my poems feel real. You felt my pain, the hurt, and witnessed the tears that dried next to the ink. You made me feel like I mattered by listening. I neglected my pen and paper years ago and recently you encouraged me to remember the pain, remember the hurt, and remember the love and place it back on paper. You are a huge reason why my dream can now rest in my hands. Thank you for being you. Thank you for the long nights reading poem after poem, pitching idea after idea, and giving me the strength to tap into parts of my heart that I struggled to address. Love you forever and always. I can't say thank you enough, Treyvon Brunson.

Big thanks to my close friends, Maranda and Shawn, for helping me edit my book. Though you both have a lot on your plate you all took the time to support me. Thank you both for being my rock. You are amazing women and I appreciate you both. Love you ladies.

I also want to thank my friends and family who have supported me in this journey by critiquing poems, uplifting me, and assisting me with whatever I needed. I thank you all so much for being there for me when you didn't have to be. Love y'all dearly.

Definitely a huge thanks to Daphnie Glenn. You helped me bring my vision to life. Thank you so much from the depth of my soul. You are truly a blessing and an inspiration.

Introduction

A child who was broken. A child who longed for peace. A child who cried every night. Cried instead of sleep. I was robbed of my memories that breathe in every child's dream. That love was a feeling that rode the sands of time. I became familiar with the deception that hid in its eyes. Love became a lesson. It became tainted and bruised. 16 years old and I had the emotions that pushed an adult to intentionally rest at the bottom of the sea. Not because I did not see the physical beauty that reflected in my presence. Not because I allowed the remarks of my peers to weaken my spirit. But because the love that was supposed to be permanent began to fade. I sat in the timid grace of loneliness and lived with the truth that if your situation is not black and white, it is not acknowledged.

I was robbed of the love that lived in my family's heart. I had to make a decision. Should I endure the hate and withstand the abuse for a chance at love and serenity? The love that I knew and worshiped my entire life. This love became rotten. It withered away like a dying rose that slowly was forgotten. It no longer welcomed peace with its presence, but instead brought pain, lies, and deceit. Some people spoke of them as evil and senseless. A small deranged army who dictated everything and everyone around them. If you dared to challenge their demands you were punished in various ways. Whether that be an object across your face or a knife against the artery that pulsated in your neck. You were isolated and only discovered when your physical and mental strength was ready to be challenged. I was told I was nothing. I was told I would go crazy. I was assured love never met my acquaintance. They used their words and various objects to pierce my skin. The irony was the words cut deeper than any knife, any metal belt hook, or physical aggression ever could. The words that ran freely from their tongue. The mischievous demeanor that enlightened you on their purpose. I was terrified, but I didn't show it. I screamed every single night questioning my life, my existence, my purpose. But they couldn't know it. Their responses were based on my strength and I was not going to let them know they were breaking me.

* * *

My heart eagerly rattled the cage in my chest that courageously protected my existence. I could not sleep. I could not miss my opportunity to leave. A gallon of water raced down my body in less than 30 minutes. That was my alarm clock. I refused to miss my opportunity. I was not going to miss my moment. Every hour I awakened like clockwork. I would peer at the end of the bed and lay back down. So far the room was filled with only me. I could hear the ants march left to right. I could hear the wind whistle as it rubbed against the leaf that laid on the ground. Fear left me attentive. It dominated my body, so I couldn't find peace. Sleep that night was only a dream.

It finally hit the hour that marked my future. Once again, I peeked at the end of my bed and I saw her. She laid on the floor like a guard dog awaiting it's next target. My heart dropped to my feet. I was not going to make it. I was terrified! I could hear the beads of sweat fall down my body and land in the sheets. The lead guard laid on the floor in the next room. She appeared to be asleep, but I wasn't persuaded. I took a deep breath, snatched the Bible off the bed and ran. I was so shaken that I did not apply deodorant. I barely brushed my teeth. I stood in the corner of the house until it was time to leave.

My steps were small, but purposeful. They lightly tapped the wooden floor piece by piece, one by one, until I met the door's acquaintance. With one last step, I flung my body out the door and never looked back. The guards who tried so hard to destroy my future didn't realize that my presence was now a memory.

My uncle and I drove into the night before the sun struck the sky. Just like that I was gone. I stared down the road as I saw my reality turn into dust. That taste of freedom I craved was counterfeit. It left me paranoid, broken, and afraid. Tears rested in the crease of my eyes as I moved further and further away from the only life I knew. Questions began to dictate my mind. Is this the beginning of something new?

Less than an hour later, we arrived at the house. I stayed here until it was time for me to be transported to my new city later that day. I tried to ignore the events that had just taken place. I wanted to pretend I was normal. I wanted to pretend I wasn't running away from a life that had abandoned me. I wanted to feel like everyone else, even for a moment.

The individuals at this new location were not strangers. Most were around my age, outside of a few children. There was only one person I wasn't familiar with. This guy seemed a little bit older than me. He went from communicating with me to punching me in the arm to challenge my physical strength. The more I could tolerate, the more blows I received. I acted as though each blow was a joke. I attempted to return the aggression with the same force that was given to me. I wanted him to know I was just as strong as I was portraying to be.

I underestimated the circumstances and found myself in a situation that challenged my well being. I saw my innocence flash before my eyes. He lifted me off the couch and began to take me to a back room. I panicked. I moved my legs back and forth as if I was having a planned seizure. Laughter began to pierce my ears at my expense. I saw that even in the company of others, I was alone. I saw faint smiles in the distance. At the end of the hall was a young man whose face grew flush with concern, but he never moved. I waited for him to fight for me. But he never did.

No one valued me! So there in that moment, once again, I had to be my own peace. I jerked and I squirmed until my body hit the floor. Why me? Even in that moment I remained strong, but it wasn't long until I fell apart.

Chapter 1: Prisoner

Prisoner

Trapped inside my soul with nothing
 but fear and disappointment to keep me company.
I've been locked away by my own feelings of pain, anger, and disbelief, With only the dream of relief.

My tears have finally dried up,
And it's only a matter of time before I face the reality,
That in actuality freedom is a fairy-tale.
Freedom is just something you dream.
An intangible feeling that encourages you
 to persevere through the fear of failure.
A scene that only sneaks in when darkness doesn't surround me.

A prisoner to the world.
An inmate to my life.
Locked up by a world blind to the image
 that rests before their eyes.
Shackles around my wrist.
Alone.
Waiting to die.
How could you say you love me and constantly ignore my cries?

Lying helpless on the floor of my cell awaiting my sentence.
Terrified of the verdict that will be delivered.
You sit and you wait until that dreaded moment approaches,
Life finally spoke and my fate was finally chosen.
No need to look back, my future is over.
Is it really necessary to live any further?
I prayed and it only brought death one step closer.

Day and night, night and day, you sit on the tainted floor of your cell, Isolated . . . but still left dreaming.

Bridget Ford

Suicide

My room is a crime scene, well was suppose to be anyway.
Yesterday was supposed to be my last day.
OD'd on pills, death was supposed to be my fate.
Attempted suicide, but death never came.
My heart raced the clock-beating like it was insane,
That's why I figured death was just late,
All I had to do was wait.
Everything hot. Everything in my body went 10 times faster.
Gave up on my life 'cause it just didn't matter.

Bridget Ford

Code Blue

Praying death to the thoughts that breathe in my mind.
A captive to the fate I entertain sometimes.
Your life speaks value,
A pure dime in its prime.
My life challenges death,
Knocks the balance from my spine.

You see me, here thinking,
Running towards the sands of time.
Moving and challenging the end,
Finding peace in goodbye.
Though the pep in my steps often finds the lie.

My hands block the sun that leaves a glow in my eyes.
My clothes cover the flesh that burned along the ride.
See love and freedom are hidden in disguise.
They're silent and equivalent to the sands that run with time. My freedom rests among the clouds in the sky,
It will keep going and going til I'm ready to die.

Bridget Ford

Tired

Give up is the constant phrase that appears in my head everyday.
While the words hold on, and be strong, float quietly away.
One has no choice but to take heed and listen,
And quickly come up with a decision.
Whether to cry or pray or wander hopelessly astray.
Considering the fact that everything is closing in on you,
Remembering the people who don't have a clue what you're going through,
Reaching the truth that nobody cares.

Looking back and digging up hidden thoughts and feelings,
Seem to scorn you and pull you farther and farther into the world of anger.
An anger so deep that nobody understands it but you.
The pain when you realize that you never were a prize to anyone,
Especially the people who you thought loved you.

Tears pour down my face, almost everyday,
Because the phrase, "I love you", seem to slowly fade away.
Until it's gone forever, and you're left with the thought of never,
Hearing those words genuinely again.

Bridget Ford

TRAPPED

I'm alone,

But I made it.

I'm happy,
But am I faking it?

Who can tell the tears that fall?
When I can't tell if I'm crying at all.

Who can find the love in my smile?
Who can spot the dent in my crown?
Who can see the pain in my chest?
Who can feel the burns on my flesh?

Who can see me breaking down?
When I can't see past my own smile.

I fool myself,
It's me who hide the truth behind the walls in my chest.
It's me who struggle to lay my burdens to rest.

Pain won't let me win,
Fear won't keep me still,
Love won't bring me peace.

At the end of the day,
No matter what comes my way,
It will always be me.

Left alone, trapped in the jealous arms of frustration.
Lying across the lap of anguish.
Crying against the shoulder of rejection.

I'm here to stay . . .
I'll never be free . . .

Bridget Ford

Private Battle

How transparent can you be,
When the people that are the closest to you seem the hardest to reach? I am different, that's a fact.
I walk with my hands behind my back.
No defense,
No strength,
No guard,
I just react.

No warning,
No peace,
No time to count to three.
I just fall without a sound.
No alert.
Lying lifeless on the ground.

You don't move.
You can't speak.
Because my struggle is hard to believe.
It's not present in your mind,
Just the same depressing story every time.

But it's the truth that I breathe.
The pain that walks with me.
The hurt that makes it hard to leave.

A prisoner to myself.
My own mind,
Leaves my body in welts.
I am the attacker.
My mind is the aggressor.
Running from myself,
But my mind is just faster.

Bridget Ford

Reported by a Blind Eye

Love,
Peace,
Fear,
And Shame.

The sad truth is
These traits, we fail to claim.
Though they breathe in each of us
We grow deaf to their presence,
Ignoring our truth, mixing our flaws with our blessings.

Despite our true feelings,
We continue to walk-- still bleeding.
We all have prayed for peace,
We all have cried ourselves to sleep,
We all have come short of His glory,
We all have done things no one will believe.

We are all human
Looking for the truth in a dark place.
Some choose to stay,
Or have no idea how to walk away.

I still find myself fighting in an empty space,
Banging on the door,
Pleading, "Please hear my case!"

But who listens to the pain of a woman who doesn't appear to be struggling?
Waiting as her cries grow faint,
When she doesn't appear to be broken.
They assume she's walking in the crystal path that's been chosen.

Blinded by material things.
Ignoring the truth that she is afraid.
Constantly gloating how she is so brave.
But when the sun goes down,
And the moon takes the spotlight,
All you know is her name.

Bridget Ford

Transparency

Standing here alone,
Uncovering life as I grow.
Reliving the stories that lay faint in the distance.
Those stories still hidden, attacking my existence.
The feelings few see.
The memories they were shocked to believe.
The love that died right before me.
Peace is a task,
A dream I crave everyday.
Love is a figment of my imagination that slowly fades away.
Acceptance is the drug that keeps me still despite the pain.
How do you view yourself?
When you look in the mirror and your image is trapped before your eyes,
Who do you see?
Does it catch you by surprise?
If your qualities became your anatomy
Would your value be more or less?
Naked to the truth.
Frantic with the news.
Finding the strength to make it through,
The truth that no one sees the weakened spirit that is a part of you.

Bridget Ford

Broken Trust

When your trust is shattered,
Is it still a foundation?
Is it an unspeakable trait that's never mentioned?
Why live your life with security hidden?
Listening to see if deceit will cloud your vision?
Or will it block your heart,
Before you let it go too far?
Will it destroy your dreams before trust is able to be conceived?
Who lives life trusting they will survive?
Despite the lie their heart is suppose to dry my eyes?
Although their actions push you to say goodbye.
When you give into the lie you become absent from reality.
You ignore the signs and obey your heart.
You wait and you manipulate your mind
  to believe you don't need trust,
Though a life without trust is an empty one.

Bridget Ford

Decrepit Love

Looking for the light in a dark place.
Praying and hoping for the day my dreams decide to stay.
Run away from the thought that stability is enough?
Lie limp at the thought of the hearts I couldn't trust?
I dismissed my once a time peace and never replaced it.
Peering at my future drowning in anguish.
Gone like the feather lost in the wind.
Crying in fear that my past is the end.
They won't peek into my future and rebirth my smile.
They won't pick up the crown they forcibly knocked down.
That happiness I can't trust, but it'll never be alone.
It will always be that broken part of me that pushes me to move forward.
Decrepit love my heart knowingly stole.

Bridget Ford

I am a prisoner to myself.
I am an inmate to my mind.

I constantly battle the idea of peace in the light of death. It felt as if the warm blood that continued to flow through my body was punishment. This so-called "life" that I continued to be a part of was a nightmare. I was alive. My eyes opened every morning. I could feel the sun on my brown skin. I could even hear my heart beat through my chest. Every time my eyes freed themselves from darkness, they were scorched by the flames of hell. I was living a dream I never asked for.

I am a prisoner to myself.
I am an inmate to my mind.
I am a captive of loneliness.

Chapter 2: Emptiness

* * *

Almost 4 am and we were still walking with the moonlight, carrying our belongings on our backs. Though I was on Acres Ave for over 4 hours, walking back and forth down an empty street, I was still excited to embrace our new future. We had made it to downtown Sumter. Within minutes we were driven by men to our destination, of which we had none. They took us to our new home at a raggedy motel that screamed rape, drugs, and body bags. Never supporting the company of strangers, I continued to be seen and not heard. I was the youngest. That mentality of the oldest knows best was immediately challenged when we were casually brought to our room. Apparently, this was the room we would share with these bodyguards. I was 17, but appeared to be 13. Yet their minds continued to wonder. You could see the tainted lust in their eyes, on their lips, and in their tone. I could see their perverted thoughts as clear as I could see the hand in front of me. Three men suddenly surrounded me. I felt like it was a dream. One man touched my thigh while the other one talked me against a wall. Two other men rested their bodies against the door frame. I couldn't outrun them without neglecting my innocence. I couldn't scream for help when in that location, no one appeared to be a victim. So I prayed silently to my Father as I closed my eyes. Almost immediately the phone rang. Briefly we were left in the room with our thoughts, our fears, and no future. With nowhere to go and no one to call, what now? Trust had abandoned me. Love had forgotten me. I was alone. No mother. No father. No protector against the afflictions of the world. No one. Just me. I felt insignificant. I lost the person that triggered my heart to beat. How was I going to make it without a foundation? How would I navigate the complexity of this unforgiving world as a child? How would I process the truth, that you didn't choose me?

Abandoned

Trust is a figment of my imagination I fail to see.
It's a deceitful, graceful creature I often believe.
It took me in its arms and promised not to leave,
Vulnerability called a truce, my presence was a tease.

That warm grip that echoed from your embrace.
The smooth lips that kissed my cheek and made my pain go away.
The love that beamed like it was yesterday.
I just wanted you to stay.

I know you felt the tear that dropped from my eyes.
I know you heard the pain I screamed as I fought with the sky.
I know you felt the fear when I had nothing left.
I know you felt the kiss when I put death to the test.

I looked for you to hold out your hand,
And shield me from the life I didn't understand.
The person who was supposed to fight til the end,
Left me at the altar like I was the sin.

You left me naked,
Without a defense.
You left me to make it,
As if death was a wish.

You killed trust and buried it deep,
You're the reason why,
Peace, I may never reach.

Bridget Ford

As a Mother

I struggle everyday,
Afraid that time may not take the pain away.
Terrified that love isn't enough.
Fearful of the future that's to come.
Because you're not here so you can't be there.
You won't be there to help me navigate life.

Why can't you love me the way it's supposed to be?
Unconditionally.
No lies, no false peace.
Just the love that should have been present from the first time you laid your eyes on me.

In 1993, you should have known you would always protect me?
Did you tell yourself that very statement on my birthday?
Or did you cry out to God since love was absent that day?

When did you decide to love me?
Why didn't it come naturally?
I have to say, even in the midst of pain I have learned a lot from the mystery of your heart,
From the confusion of your tears and the uncertainty that lived in your touch.
You never really knew how to feel about me.
Since my life did not bring you peace.

My life interrupted your future,
Making love hard to see.
So do I understand the misplacement of your heart?
Of course I do. I always have.
But as a mother myself, I will never understand.

Bridget Ford

Motherly Love

Broken, beaten, and bruised.
No comfort, you left my wounds to ooze.
Ooze a pain so thick that only love can fix.
That motherly love, that nurses you when you're emotionally sick.
She holds you when she senses you're going through,
She nurtures you when you don't have a clue what to do,
She takes on your burdens so you won't have to.
She protects you the best way she can,
From the cruelty of the world.
Safe in her arms like the eye of the storm.
Serene visions are the scenes that form.
Reassuring you that you don't have to hide anymore.

Bridget Ford

On my Own

You left me here alone,
To deal with life on my own.
You're gone but still present,
Feel the stories untold.

My heart has been removed,
I'm stuck not knowing what to do.
I'm afraid, I mentally, will not make it through.

I can't control my thoughts,
I can't mute my mind.
I have to find a way to take it,
So I won't mess up every time.

I battle within myself.
I'm my own enemy.
I know what I must do,
But I don't have it in me.

Walk away from the love?
Be okay with the lies?
Run away from the fears?
Lie deaf from the cries?

I cry out in pain, now every other day.
I'm scared to embrace it, because the pain may remain.

I'm weak but I hide it.
The pain? Y'all ignore it.
So it's me, here alone, learning life on my own.

Bridget Ford

Forced Independence

Who do you run to when everyone is gone?
Who do you call when no one will pick up the phone?
It's you still wondering how you'll make it on your own.
With a baby on your back searching for a place to call home.

No family, no friends.
Just you, fighting til the end.
This battle called life is as deadly as a sin.
It eats you and beats you leaving you with no defense.
You're here all alone, searching for strength on your own.

You have to find your peace,
And continue to fight for freedom.
You have to learn the ropes,
And be there for those still sleeping.

My peace is in her heart,
My love lies near her bosom,
My trust fell at her feet,
Her uncertainty stole the air that I breathe.
How could she be so unsure about me?

I still need you to be free.
I still need you to be me.
I know our eyes have become blind to the person before us,
But it's not too late to see me for who I've grown to be.

See me for me.
That's all I ever wanted,
Was for you to notice me.
Love me unconditionally.
They say true love is strong enough to make a blind man see.
Try it again on me.

Bridget Ford

Concealed Sadness

My arms and my legs remained tangible to the eye.
My focus and vision remained in the sky.
My mind was gone.
My hope transgressed,
My future was challenged once my heart undressed.

You silenced the voice that played in your ear.
Verbal communication became a new fear.
It could be the moment that solidified my fate,
So I placed my heart,
My feelings,
And my truth on paper and watched you witness my escape.

I absorbed your glances and gazes,
Emotionless to my dismay.
Your eyes were consumed with emptiness,
An emptiness that chose to stay.

It's smug brash stare challenged me,
I saw pain that rested in the tunnel of your dark brown eyes.
It peeked from the corner of your pupil as if it wanted to make it right.

In those moments I laid my pain at your feet.
I saw your hurt. I witnessed your pain.
Just like me,
You were lost, confused, and afraid.

A sadness stared back at me I couldn't describe.
As my words grew faint and my heart began to cry.
A strong black girl who's pain I couldn't hide,
I will die in this place if my freedom is denied.

I saw in that moment you were mentally gone
 and you weren't coming back.
I walked with my head held high even though
 my spine showed through my back.
You wanted to be my rock but those thoughts declared,
Love was enough,
Even if it wasn't fair.

Your knight, your armor, your hero without a cape.
I could have been your peace,
I just needed you to stay.
Stay mentally and emotionally with me,
But depression was displayed.
I prayed to God for death to find me,
But my peace never came.

Bridget Ford

Butchered Love

Robbed of the feeling that rests in my heart,
Blind to the memory of love hidden in the dark.
A peace that only came when the light didn't shine.
A love that only spoke when nobody was around.
To give you my all and lay it in your hands.
To give you the heart, you failed to understand.
The peace that could grow from one simple memory,
The love that could've sparked from one piece of honesty.
Who am I to you?
When the city begins to rest.
To lay your eyes upon me, I'm standing in the flesh.
The love you butchered each day and laid it at my feet,
Became the wings beneath my arms that I still can't believe.

Bridget Ford

Superwoman

Quiet yet unique,
From your head to your feet.
Your intelligence,
Your beauty,
Was the light that summoned me.

A woman on her own without a man to lead,
Made me see the strength that became a part of me.

I am an extension of you,
I hope your eyes can see,
And feel,
And touch,
The heat that engulfs me.

I am a force just like the woman I knew.
A ball of energy who demands respect in a room.
I am your prodigy.
I am your vision.
I am the woman you made me before my peace went missing.

You made me into the woman I am today.
Integrity,
Love,
Intelligence.
A strong black woman I'm afraid.

You are my hero,
Without the cape and the vest.
A superhuman whose blood runs the same in my chest.

A woman who held the pressures of the world,
And did her best to try to make it.
Battled through the storms.

A superwoman nonetheless, but a woman just the same.
It's your strength and integrity that is stained in my name.
A diamond in disguise.
The world's personal blessing,
To meet a real angel God sent straight from heaven.

Bridget Ford

Chapter 3: Hope

* * *

      We ran until our feet no longer chastised the pavement. In seconds, we were able to rearrange the entire room of the motel. Any furniture that was not secured to the floor now stood in front of the door that divided us from 2 men. They fought with the door that defended my innocence. They rocked it and rattled it for 20 minutes. I was terrified, but I had no time to entertain the belief that the furniture was not enough. Every push and every shove the men exercised towards our lifeless bodyguard, constantly opened a crack that was wide enough for us to see our potential fate. I was 17. Still a child. Still a baby. So far from understanding the dismantling troubles this world brings without a second thought.

      The door rocked back and forth. The hinges screamed at the resistance it continued to experience. Then suddenly the battle stopped. My knees dung into my chest as I listened for the next sound that would alert me of my fate. I watched the men gaze into the motel room like two hyenas salivating over it's next prey. Finally they disappeared into the night. My eyes beamed into the moonlit room for hours. How can I leave this room when I wasn't sure of my fate? Their bodies could be posted around the corner, waiting for me to let my guard down. I sat in fear until I had enough courage to remove the furniture from the door and tackle my future.

      My determination was low, but not nonexistent. "I can make it. I can do this". I welcomed the cold nights. I embraced the hunger. I knew that depression was ready to captivate my life. Even then I would not give up. I had to sacrifice the life I knew for my peace. I had to walk away so death would no longer befriend me. Though that decision was the best for my life, it still left me broken.

Hope

Embracing the heartache,
Respecting the pain,
Challenging the peace,
That will bring better days.

Hope is now here,
Staring at me face to face,
Motivating me to persevere through this dry and desert place.

I pray without words,
And cry without tears,
Because I know that one day the end will be near.

I know I want better,
This was not a debate.
These were the days I was left dreaming,
 even though I was awake.

Happiness becomes my lifestyle.
Joy becomes routine.
I no longer have to fit in with the lies in-between.

Peace is now my truth.
Hope is now my friend.
Joy is now reality,
I no longer have to pretend.

Bridget Ford

Blurred Happiness

The kiss of the sun on your smooth skin.
The touch of your newborn baby tucked purposely
between your arm and your breast.
The whisper of love's gentle voice as it dances helplessly
around your weakened heart.
Or the sound of a mother making the words "I love you" breathe
it's first breath across the deserted sky.

What is happiness to the new mom trying to find her way?
What is happiness to the child who doesn't have a place to
stay?
Does happiness live with love?
Does happiness exist with peace?
What is happiness if joy still hasn't heard your plea?

Happiness is more than a song.
It's more than a moment.
It depends on how you define it.

Happiness is
A peace you can't control.
A love that may grow old.
A moment that rests in your soul.
Happiness stands alone.

It's different from peace,
Because it's not present when you sleep.
It moves to its own beat.
Kind of like you and me.
Happiness is different, beautiful, but unique.

Bridget Ford

Last Through the Seasons

Through the cool autumn's breeze,
Through the silent summer's sneeze,
Through the young and playful trees,
Be there when the clouds freeze.

Be there through the ups.
Be present when life's tough.
Be waiting at the end, when I decide to run.

I can't see my future,
'Cause my past memories fade.
The people I know and love will one day walk away.
Dreaming of a love that's present despite the pain.

Every year.
Season to season.
The same love, no one different.

But I'm different.
Different from the rest.
My heart beats for love,
Their hearts were always blessed.

Blessed with the presence of love that awakened their smile.
The love that you can trust, that'll never knock you down.
I was cursed with the charge to figure it out.
Basking in the love that faded in the crowd.

I await real love that breathes through the seasons,
That's always present,
That never goes missing.
True love,
That gives life its meaning.

Bridget Ford

Left in the Night

Contemplating peace.
Gambling jagged sleep.
Pushing for a life that didn't surround me.

Running from myself.
Shaking, cold with welts.
My naked body battered and bruised,
Lying helpless against the cold pavement.

Lying at the foot of the world.
Crying, begging for a chance to explore.
A life without misery,
A wish that was ignored.

The pavement was there to break my fall.
It wasn't concerned,
Never kept me warm,
But it was present unlike the rest.

It watched my body shake every night.
Listened as my dreams died every time I closed my eyes.
A prisoner to the world as if breathing was a crime.

Fighting for a life that died over time,
Praying to a God whose presence was implied.
Why find strength when his truth was a lie?

Laying on the cold pavement like a corpse in the sea.
Lifeless,
Still breathing,
Searching for peace.

That one faint light was enough for me.
To get up, reset, and chase my dreams.

Bridget Ford

Royalty Just the Same

Trust is a character I can't perceive,
An old fable that comes alive in my dreams,
A relationship so sweet, yet cowardly and mean.

It lies to you and cuddles you,
Until it finds what it needs.
Once it steals your innocence,
It packs up and leaves.

See trust betrays your heart,
It befriends you when you're alone in the dark,
Then slowly and steadily it rips your peace apart.

It captures your thoughts,
And fades your smile.
It silences your laugh,
And rebirths a frown.
It taunts the day you let your guard down.
But even then it'll never steal your crown.

Bridget Ford

Seasoned Wisdom

As my eyes brush across my wrinkled skin,
And my battered heart reflects in my smile.
As my face greets the sunlight,
And my mind gets lost in the clouds.

I reflect on the life I knew.
The one most rarely see.
The peace I once had in front of me.
The one I was forced to leave.

I see the children running in the night.
I see adults laughing as their smiles beam.
I see the elders in the distance,
Stuck in a repeated scene.

They take in the love among them.
The family that can't see.
The love that moves mountains.
The love allowing us to breathe.

Elders dissect the truth,
Within the living souls.
They can see the pain,
That makes my body numb, fragile, and cold.

It's a part of who I am, but remains hidden in the light.
Denounced by Love, now a continuous fight.
The pain that dictates my face like a mask with a smile.
The love that died in my arms next to hope after trial.

Pain teases my presence,
And rebirths the lesson,
That my pride would not allow.

The elders eagerly remind me what my God is all about.
They awaken my spirit with that one simple song.
That captures my soul and holds me all night long.
It's the love and wisdom that shows in their steps.
That if you stand fast and hold true,
God's love, peace, and joy will find you.

Bridget Ford

Innocent Dreams

The man at the altar awaiting your smile.
The love that fell from the trees and the clouds.
The music that danced with the elegant wind.
That sways with the crowd with a clever grin.

Can you see the roses in the meadows alive and vibrant?
That whistle with the acceptance of the love witnessed often.
The beautiful white dress that embraces every curve,
From the small curve of my back to the dip in my waist,
The dress dashingly complements each curve with lace.
All white. Embroidered. With a train that never stops.

Our vows to each other light up the night.
Awakens my heart, forcing tears in my eyes.
I smile and I giggle at the love it invites.
I woke up and vowed,
This love I dare to see.
I placed it in my pocket and ran with the belief,
That one day this dream could finally be me.

Bridget Ford

I Deserve It

The hands on the clock were silent but it knew,
It teased me and laughed and barely began to move.
My heart began to pound,
My feet broke a sweat.
Almost 10 o'clock and our voices have not met.
My very best friend who always stole the night.
My own personal guard who was late but on time.
He listened to me bring each story to life.
He laughed with me,
Making me no longer want to fight.
The battle of trust.
His focus and attention made me see he was different.
My rock for many years before his place was ever
mentioned. My foundation for 11 who made my
dreams come true, Pushing me everyday,
By expressing the message I refused to say.
Protecting me with his words,
From the life I once observed.
Reminding me that I am royalty,
I am chosen,
And the life I lived in my dreams . . . I DESERVE IT.
Late and afraid, but my future, I AM WORTH IT.

Bridget Ford

The Beauty of a Man

A support that was tangible.
A love that spoke loud.
A peace that was gentle, that rebirthed my smile.

The beauty behind a man,
Though some fail to understand,
A man behind his woman,
To help her and hold her when she stumbles.

Who knew a love, so fresh yet pure.
So callus, yet supple.
Could be my peace, when I couldn't find the air to breathe.

My hopes fluttered into the sympathetic scene of a world I could not process.
This man gave me the hope I neglected to find.
He loved me and cared for me despite the lie.
He gifted me the motivation of time.

The beauty of a man.
The love that graced his hands.
The hope that became my legs to stand.

It was then, I knew.
A future could be true.
Because his love for me, was as strong as the sea,
So my dreams and hopes I could now believe.
The beauty of a man became my eyes to see,
The motivation that was always a part of me.

Bridget Ford

I challenged myself to find the strength that seemed
absent.
Hope was tangible, yet a fairytale.
The tiny bit of motivation that rested among
the stars encouraged me to entertain peace.
I searched for hope in my future.
I called out for it in my dreams.
I even looked to God as I got on my knees.
I searched for something that was always right beside
me. It was living in the vessel of another human being.
I am human and despite what I choose to believe,
I need someone to help me stand.
I was falling and they broke my fall.
They reminded me of who I am and who I choose to be.

Chapter 4: Chasing Peace

Two large garbage bags and a overpacked bookbag and we were on our way! So many items I had already left behind, but it got me one step closer to freedom. The glimpse of freedom in my dreams wasn't enough. I could see it now. The light behind the mountain. I could finally kiss the dreadful motel room goodbye. I would no longer have to witness my neighbors as they sloopingly sold their distasteful figures to the highest bidder. I would be free from the aggressive behaviors of men who studied my staggered routine. My undeveloped plan was as perfect as the forgotten pearl resting at the bottom of the sea. It pushed me to want more. It pushed me to believe that one day I would make it.

From Sumter, SC to Columbia, SC we traveled in style on the Greyhound bus. A system I never knew existed before this moment. We dragged our garbage bag of clothes, shoes, and personal items down the aisle until we found our seat. I could smell freedom. I could touch love. I could hear the laughter as we headed to Job Corp. Job Corp would rebirth my future. A new job! A fresh start! At this point, $7.00 an hour sounded like the deal of a lifetime. The opportunities Job Corp offered were better than my reality. I saw freedom sitting on the horizon like the radiant sun when it first opens its eyes. Happiness was only a bus stop away. Once we arrived we walked from the bus terminal to Job Corp, gracing the hot pavement with our elegant luggage. After hours of speaking with the manager, we were told that I could not stay as I was still a minor.

Darkness engulfed the sky. After the manager's laughter ceased, he personally drove us back to the motel in Sumter, SC. When he drove off, disappointment dictated my face. I was humiliated. I was failing every class for 3 weeks for this very moment. For a broken opportunity. Hunger was now routine. Panties and bras had now diminished. I had nothing and just like that, my dreams and motivation ceased. Darkness captivated my body. Pain striked by chest. Love became a test. I was fighting for a freedom I couldn't believe. I was praying for a future that once wasn't a dream. WHY WAS THIS HAPPENING TO ME? I could not and would not rationalize this. He loves me. I know he does. So why me? Why would you do this to me? Tears ran down my cheeks like an angry mob ready for revenge. When I finally opened my eyes, Moment for Life by Nicki Minaj echoed throughout the small motel room. I dried my eyes and declared my freedom. "I can do this!"

Strength of a Woman

Strength is in the woman with no legs to stand.
Strength is in the woman who's tears lie in her hand.
Strength is in the woman who cries herself to sleep.
Strength is in the woman who suffers from defeat.
Strength is in the woman who no longer chooses to fight.
Strength is in the woman whose life is out of sight.
Strength is in the woman, no shame in goodbye.
Strength is in the woman who seemed to live a lie.
Strength is in a woman who falls or who stands.
Strength is in the woman who doesn't understand.
Strength is in the woman you can see it in her eyes.
Strength is in the woman, it's too strong for her to hide.
Strength is in the woman from her head to her feet.
A strength that is visible even when it's hard to see.

Bridget Ford

Light in Darkness

Stuck in a world blind to your truth,
Crying every night not knowing what to do.
Pressure and pain refuses to move,
Me here alone horribly confused.

Sitting in misery but focused nonetheless,
The feelings of freedom against the thoughts of distress.
Begging and crying Lord please make me next,
My time is coming, my chance to be blessed.

I ran into a peace so stingy and creed,
It held me and shook me and forced me to leave.
A love hate relationship that was tough but warm,
It put me in mess but sheltered me when it stormed.

It knocked me to my feet,
Then helped me off the floor,
The thorn to my rose,
That never let me sleep.

It awoke my bitterness,
That pushed me to reach,
For the stars in the sky that no man could see.

Peace took my hand when love didn't grow,
It brushed me off, sat me up, then taught me control.
My headache and my drive that brought me back to life.
The captain of my ship that forced me to try.

Bridget Ford

Cries Never Heard

Drowning in my mind,
Only sometimes,
Do I meet the chill of death,
   in the middle of sunshine.

Fear and pain both one in the same,
A cold dark secret I fail to maintain.

Tears freeze,
Water ceased,
But the pain in my chest continues to beat.

Looking at the shackles longing to be free,
That chosen peace that I may never reach.
My own mental freedom starts within me.

One foot in the dirt while the other rests in the sand,
Torn between peace and the crooked nails on a dark hand.

Peace is what you chose without ever forming words,
Peace is what you declare even when it sounds absurd,
Peace is a dream that forces me to leave.

Trapped inside a bubble.
The journey to peace,
 A silent struggle.

Bridget Ford

Silent & Deadly

Who said words can't bruise?
As sharp as any weapon left to bear the bad news.
One shot from betrayal,
Two shots from deceit,
Three shots from love, whose aid you once received.

Words are weapons that are silently cruel.
A pain that lives on its own belief.
A bully that forces its opponents to retreat.
Words will slowly beat a man until anger and confusion puts his soul to sleep.
It'll cut him up and burn his body as he cries out for peace.

Words are the truth behind the lie.
More powerful than we believe.
The cuts produced by a silent sword.
Illegitimate life somehow breathes.
A modest deceit and pain that can knock you on your knees.

Bridget Ford

Fool's Gold

Looking towards the light at the end of the war,
Running towards a thought I wish to explore,
Leaning towards a dream that breathes in the light,
Praying for the kiss of happiness before I close my eyes.

The rainbow at the end that resides in our mind,
Composed of happiness and peace, a beautiful design.
The love we saw as clear as the sky,
The love we mourn when the dream starts to die.

We look to the hills,
We look at the light,
We rest in its presence,
Though the light burns our eyes.

We stand and we fight til death brings us home,
Because life is full of hate so love we must explore.

To touch the hand of the ones you love and rest in their smile,
You find peace in their presence even though you're bleeding out.
To look death in the eyes and greet him with a grin,
Because this life he interrupts has now become your friend.

To make it to the rainbow that made you gaze into the sky,
Makes it okay to meet your master as you wave your hands goodbye.
Running towards a myth,
That may or may not exist.

Broken at the truth,
The kiss of happiness?
May not include you.

Bridget Ford

Only Time Will Tell

Only time will tell how my life will be.
Only time will tell how long I will sustain peace.
Only time will tell when my tears will fall.
Only time will tell if I'm going to make it at all.

Only time can glimpse into my future,
And only time can provide motherly nurture.
Time has the ability to strengthen, protect, and prepare me for the journey that's next,
Because only time knows best.

Bridget Ford

Memories

Photo albums, videos, and scrapbooks.
Memories are there enticing you to take a look.
Seducing you to reminisce on the past,
On those moments you took captive, so that it would last.

You neglect the happiness that surrounds you.
You expand the memories that reflect what you went through.
You scream silently to friends, "they don't have a clue",
I know love is all you pursue.

Those moments.
Those memories that fell at your feet.
The thoughts and joys that allowed you to breathe.
Lives in your mind even when you grow weak.

It's the love in the smile of the man you once loved,
It's the peace in the eyes from the one that sits above,
The dreams that are rebirthed from one simple memory,
Puts your mind and your body in a state of serenity.

See peace and love those moments invite,
That push me and encourage me to fight the doubt in time,
A love that lasts forever, no peace in goodbye,
Thoughts into memories that'll never really die.

The laugh from a mother as they hold you in their arms.
The memories you took captive so again you could explore.
It's the love in their eyes that in that moment you neglect,
The love you once had, now a memory is what's left.

The love in their eyes, I wish I could restore.
The laughter in the smiles I can't seem to ignore.
Those hidden memories I can't seem to reach.
Once forgotten moments that allowed my mind to sleep.

Bridget Ford

Hidden Desires

What is your heart's passion?
What do you dream that keeps you wanting to modify reality?
Is it true love's first kiss?
Is it success in your career?
Is it peace from within?
Do all three serenade your thoughts at night?
Do all three give you a kiss goodnight?
Do all three remain a dream,
Hidden from the sun,
Sitting in the loneliness of the shade you can't trust?
Basking in the air of uncertainty,
Can they be your truth?
Or will it stay hidden like the stars behind the moon?
Your dreams, your thoughts, shine bright
But fail to come through.
Room full of people yet no one else is in the room.
You focus on your strengths and embrace your weaknesses,
You shelter your dreams while your heart is still bleeding,
So far from peace, but no one believes me.
Living in reality yet my mind is still dreaming.

Bridget Ford

One Wish

False hope.
A repeated dream.
A shattered wish I'll never see.

The love of a mother,
Applauding in the pew.
The touch of a woman I knew before two.
The light that shines in the bay, as love takes its true form.

The embrace of a mother
A touch I once explored.
But here I sit,
Awaiting love's true form.

Pondering thoughts I once knew,
Wishing for true loves touch from a woman.
A woman who knew me before two.

A woman who loved me as I irresponsibly broke the rules.
The breath of a woman on my neck,
That chastises me with love nonetheless.
I was robbed of that feeling a long time ago,
Watched love die before me and lose its glow.

Love became death,
Love became cruel,
Love became a feeling I began to choose.

No pulse, No life.
It's relevance now hidden in strife.
A battered dream I now ignored.
So I built it.

Hand by hand.
Step by step.
Until the people I loved became a board of chess.
See now you can leave and I'll wish you the best,
Because true love,
Real love,
I'll never possess.

Bridget Ford

The Rock Behind the Glass

Reach into my heart and reveal what's inside,
Feel the love in the dark,
Let it dry your glistening eyes.
Separate your heart from the past.
Be here just you, alive in the moment.
Separate from reality.
Isolated from your thoughts.
Just you,
Your peace,
The love that wrapped around you in the dark.
Be your own peace,
Snuggle in its arms.
Allow your love to encompass you.
Allow your love to grow with you.
Let your love be your peace.
Let it live beyond your dreams.
Allow yourself to be all you need.

Bridget Ford

Growth

What do you do when you're tired of feeling lonely?
Where do you go when your heart is not open?
Why do you continue to struggle on your own?
You, left alone, because your plea grew old.

Tucked away in your own mental closet,
Holding the burden your brain cannot process,
Reaching for clues that someone is there,
Ignoring the feeling that nobody cares.

That space you sit when the world seems cold.
It may not be pretty, but it's yours. It knows.
It holds you and listens,
The peace before the storm.

It degrades and embraces, you must be warned.
Darkness brings awareness making you mindful of what you see.
Peace and true love is not always guaranteed.
Darkness is a curse yet a blessing in disguise,
For it's the struggle in the dark that opens your eyes.

It will get better.
Cliches in all your thoughts you'll master.
One day at a time, your peace you'll soon find.
Once you realize you're the reason you're so far behind.

Bridget Ford

Just Be Still

Happiness.
To sit in the arms of peace.
To hear the crickets sing its song throughout the night.
To see love lay beside me one more time.
Feel the warm embrace of the sheets wrapped around my body.
To watch the moon shine it's light on those searching for a message in the sky.
To feel the love that filled your eyes.

Happiness.
The moment of peace.
The peace that entered when I rested in the arms of the Lord who comforts me.
Peace came and engulfed me.
When I decided to be still and listen.

Listen to the baby cry into the night.
Listen to the darkness as it dries it's weeping eyes.
Listen to the breeze that bears witness to the lie.
Remember the love that awoke your smile?
The love you felt though silent,
Vowed to never knock you down.

Don't forget the peace that glistened in your smile
Dreaming of your peace, your love, your joy.
Be still and wait.
Be still. Have faith.
Just be still and listen . . .

Bridget Ford

A Song's Embrace

Laying on the mattress that gently caresses my body.
Surrendering my thoughts to the rhythm of the music that gracefully moves to each beat.
Music prepares my escape.
Without warning it takes me to a better place.
It loves me and cares for me,
Even throws punches when anger surrounds me.
Music is the friend that listens through the night.
It's my tissue when I can't wipe my eyes.
Music removed the gun when I was ready to die.
Nothing in this world can take away the pride,
I hold in my friend, who depends on notes as it's disguise.
Music is peace,
Music summoned sleep,
Music removed the darkness that broke me.
As the tears roll down my face,
And my heart grips the seat,
I knew I would find peace,
Once I allowed music to be a part of me.

Bridget Ford

Friendship

Dreaming in a world that doesn't stop, doesn't breathe, doesn't slow down.
Standing in traffic listening to noise that fails to make a sound.
Just me and my thoughts awaiting someone like you,
The woman who became my family before I had a clue.
You slid into my life and captured my heart,
You gave me what I was missing,
The family that fell apart.
The smile that stretches across my skin, began with you as my friend,
And now time has made us so much more than this.
My sister, my mom, the joy beneath my eyes,
My dawg who won't hesitate to be my shoulder, when I'm ready to cry.
My confidant,
My truth,
My rock when I'm confused,
You help maintain my peace,
The love you share with me,
Allows us both to grow beyond the trees.
Thank you for being my light when I couldn't see.
Despite your reservations,
You have become a huge part of the peace that finally found me.

Bridget Ford

Love

Love is callus.
Love is worn.
Love is a female you'll never learn.

Love can be beautiful.
It can also be unique.
It can be as silent as the clouds watching me.

Love can be an enemy,
Love can be a friend,
Love can be the curse disguised but a sin.

This love fooled me and held me just the same.
This love knocked me down and carried out it's name.
Despite the rain it brought,
Despite the tears it saw,
Love lifted me up above the sky.

Love looked me in my eyes and vowed to never lie,
Then as quickly as it said it, that love began to die.
It's that love that kept my ears to the sky.
It taught me to find peace in the love that tries.

Real love isn't perfect,
It's flawed just like the rest.
But it's conditions are limitless,
Like the heart against my breast.

God blessed it from above,
Brought it to my feet,
He allowed me to pick,
The love from my dreams.

He summoned it's grace, let it rest in my hands,
Pushed me every day to fight, though I didn't understand.
Love is insane, but it's beauty's as vocal as the message hidden in the rain.
It birthed the hope, that pushed me closer to the smile behind the frame.

Bridget Ford

Comprehension of Peace

It took me a long time to get here.
But by the grace of God I made it.
I made it to the land of contentment,
To the sea of peace,
That's built off the broad understanding of the brash disdainment they share towards me.

I'm no longer searching for love in their hearts.
I'm no longer trying to aid the pain that screams.
I'm okay with no longer loving you.
I'm at peace with the shattered dream.
Today is the day that hope is dismissed.
Today is the day I mentally leave.

I'm at peace with the reality of you.
The pain and tears that ran down my face,
I will no longer bleed for you.
I release you from the place you had in my heart,
You're no longer present, you're like the dust in the stars.
Maybe one day time will help me heal,
But until then there will always be a scar,
That marks the day my heart shed its first tear.

Bridget Ford

They say what is understood doesn't have to be explained, like the unspoken love that proudly wraps around the hearts of newly weds.

Or the joy that floods the room at the sight of a newborn baby.
The expected is understood, while the unimaginable is neglected.
I lived a life that was not ideal.
As a result, peace became a fantasy.
I began to degrade myself with the world.
The peace I craved at the end of the journey seemed unfamiliar, unattainable, and unreal.

Words began to attack me in every encounter.
I was lost and forgotten, chasing a peace I wasn't sure I would find.
My mind was my first enemy.

It was filled with guilt, fear, anger, and hurt that interfered with the level of serenity that I desired.

I had to rise above the pain so I could rest among the clouds.
I had to make a conscious decision to obtain peace.

Chapter 5: Self-Made

      Bridget Ford echoed across the screen revealing my Master's in Nursing. I screamed! The day had finally come when I could hold my head up high and say I did it. Many would say I already hold the title of an accomplished African American woman, but to me, I am just getting started. My heart still ached at the thought that over 10 years later, the love I experienced growing up had not been recaptured. It had not died, just faded. I used the pain and hurt to push me to surpass my dreams. Self- Made. I am an African American woman who despite the odds, despite the misconceptions, grew into the woman I knew I could be. I am almost fearless. I am courageous. I am stronger than ever before, but I am still aware of the portion of my heart that misses the love that's supposed to be permanent.

      10 years deep and it's just me, my husband, and my baby boy. Am I surrounded by friends and some family? Of course. But do I really belong? You see love has levels. The extent of acceptance varies among the title and relationship. Though I do share the support of friends and some family, I am and will always be on the outside looking into their beautiful glass home. The elegance comes from their unconditional love they share for one another that will remain steady throughout the seasons. Peace does not always warrant an extravagant ending, but instead it offers the opportunity for new beginnings. I still battle loneliness. I still plead for peace. I still find myself fighting in my dreams. Peace is a process, as well as a choice. It takes some time to achieve, but once it's accomplished it's yours.

Here I stand

I stand before you,
A wounded soul.
Walking in pain that'll never show.

I stand before you,
With a broken heart,
A heart that once beat without being forced to start.

Here I stand before you,
Alone and cold,
Awaiting the one ready to wrap his arms around me in the pure white snow.

Here I stand before you,
Drenched in tears,
The ones that don't show,
The ones that hide my fears.

Here I stand,
Scared to death,
That peace won't find me,
I'll never be next.

Here I stand,
Can't you hear me screaming?
The dreary sounds of a broken spirit you heard echoing in the night.
The loud cries that lay faint that made you open your weary eyes.
Though still blind to the thief who stole her mind.

Here I stand before you,
Lost and confused,
Still searching for the truth,
In emotional abuse.

Bridget Ford

Who Comforts Me?

Who comforts me?
Outside of the walls that watch me sleep?
It's your thoughts, your discretions that bury me!
I am hidden like the sap beneath the bark of a tree.
Waiting and hoping for the sun to shine its light on me.
I am here,
Despite your selfish ways.
I am present.
Present to speak,
Present to see,
The emptiness that taunts me.
Who comforts me?
Who holds me?
Who dries my eyes before the tears are seen.
I am my husband.
I am my friend.
I am my mother.
I am my kin.
I am whoever I need to be.
Because I am the one who comforts me.

Bridget Ford

Journey to Peace

Strength can help you navigate the alleys of life.
Pain will keep you hidden from the memories of time.
Trust will disappear without ever saying goodbye.
Because love is not permanent in this game of life.

Hold tight and don't let go of the pain that brought your body to the floor.
Feel the pain,
Hear the lies,
Let it run through your veins and settle in your cries.

Let your past be your vision.
Let the fear last a season.
Let your strength be the rose that grows from the sand.
Let God be the lion that walks with you hand in hand.

Let Him fight your battles,
Let Him absorb your fears,
Let Him break you down,
So you can peacefully release the tears.

Let Him be your father,
Let Him be your peace,
Let Him hold you at night,
Leave your problems at his feet.

You have to release the pain that clutters your mind.
You have to be at peace with the fall that broke your spine.
You have to heal from the words that pierced your skin.
You have to forgive yourself for the thoughts you yelled within.

Silence won't keep you.
Love won't free you.
And joy won't sustain you.

True peace comes from within,
So please be you,
Let the Lord comfort you,
Address the pain and watch God move.
After all only He knows how to save you.

Bridget Ford

Beauty from Within

Rest in the beauty of life that warms your heart.
Continue to strengthen your peace when you're alone in the dark.
Be silent but loud,
Gentle but tough,
Be the person you want to be especially when it's rough.

Be the best you in the storm.
Be the star near the moon.
Be someone's peace who summoned death before they had a clue.

Be as transparent as the water that rushes on the coast of the pacific.
Be clear and free but a warden to your mystery.
Let their minds wonder and get lost in the sea.

Be as strong as a lion.
As gentle as a bird.
Be you in turmoil,
I know it sounds absurd.

But it's important to remember,
You are beautiful just the same.
Despite the fears and misconceptions,
You are the grace, the rock, the beauty behind the name.

Bridget Ford

Written Therapy

Poems lock in my truth,
And expose my heart.
They keep those moments captive,
That mentally blinded me from the start.

My poems are my peace.
They are my friend.
They hide my feelings and protect my heart,
By helping me battle the demons within.

My paper listens while my pen speaks,
My hands glide while my thoughts control me.
I bury my soul with a ballpoint pen bold,
I massage my heart and watch my truth unfold.

I allow my pen to soak up my hurt,
To absorb my fears,
And displace my tears,
I sit helplessly as it gently but purposely reveals my pain,
whispers my sorrows, and extracts the shame,
Leaving my body empty and hollow.

My poems speak volumes.
They say what my mouth refuses to form.
They become my umbrella in an unexpected storm.
My poems are my release,
they push me one step closer to being mentally free.

Bridget Ford

Assured Peace

I no longer have to worry.
I no longer have to fear.
God said, "Don't be in a hurry".
Just wait, "I'm right here".

He has it all in his hands.
He knows exactly what to do.
He's the one that made the plan,
Before your problems knew you.

Let your mind be silent,
And your heart be at ease.
Let your thoughts be vibrant,
Remove all your insecurities.

Allow Him to wrap you in His arms, hold tight, and
never let go.
You're His child, so just know, you will never be alone.

Let God be your peace.
He will protect you 'til the end.
He's my rock,
My shield,
My very best friend.

Bridget Ford

Be Present

Life is too serious to not find the humor in it.
Life would be dull if you couldn't mix some fun with it.

Relax. Breathe twice.
Live each day like it's your last.
Be here, be present,
Don't treat life like it's a task.

Stop what you're doing and take a mental picture of the moment that's invited you.
The friends that enjoy spending time with you.
The family that would be lost without you.

Drown in the beauty life brings that knocks you off your feet.
Bask in the memory of the one who made your heart skip a beat.

Don't waste precious moments worrying about a future you can't see.
Be here,
Be present,
Have faith and leap.

Fall into your destiny.
Laugh even in the pain.
Because I promise, everyone experiences hurt,
Even if it's not the same.

Be grateful you're still breathing.
Soak in every touch of the sun.
Because one day it will be over.
So be blessed now, even though it's tough.

Bridget Ford

It's Only a Test

We all have a path that whispers our name.
We all seek peace but arrive in different ways.
Though our present reflects the journey that's next,
We still find ourselves struggling to do our best.

Through the tears and the fears,
Through the prayers that we share,
We sit and we cover the truth that was always quite there.
Though God provides us with the strength to move forward,
We fear that one day the door won't be open.
The path that you've chosen is just that, a dream.

A memory that we ponder only when we're asleep.
We fill our minds with our memories of the past,
We allow ourselves to fall in the palm of life's hands,
Only to reflect on moments we failed to understand.

We are placed in situations only for a season,
To learn the true meaning of every single Christmas.
It's through those moments that we find our reason,
To sit still and wait on life's true meaning.

You are loved,
You are blessed,
Be in good cheer for this is only a test.
Before you know it that time will end,
And you will find yourself once again in the presence of those you missed.

Bridget Ford

My Purpose

Built not bought.
Here not used.
Purposely in this position I calculated with precision.

My steps are intentional.
My love is unconditional.
My trust is unreal,
As beautiful as a mermaid, that's only ideal.

I laugh with reservations.
I move with a plan.
A chair positioned beside me,
Understand I meant to stand.

Every move is calculated,
My thoughts are unique,
The love I share before you are the shoes beneath my feet.

The foundation of my world,
The pulse of my being,
The decree I was given,
That structured my existence.

Give you the very best of me,
Be your cushion when you fall,
Be the love that stands before you,
When you feel like giving up.

I am here to be your peace,
Allow me to be your rock,
I'll try my best to hold you up when the rain refuses to stop.

Everything is calculated.
Every step is intentional.
I move to help you,
To replace the love that went missing.

Bridget Ford

Justified Peace

When your journey has come to an end.
And the light now blinds your eyes.
What thoughts will flood your head?
What truth will you leave behind?

Was love a beautiful memory or a simple task that received a check?
Can you hold your head up high and say you've learned from every test?
When will you decide that it's okay for life's surprise?
When will you acknowledge the truth, that we all must someday close our eyes?

Who will you seek from the depths of your heart?
Is it love or were you destined to always be apart?
How will you divide your truth from your dreams?
How will you leave this world?
Mentally together or generously mean?

Will you have healed the wounds that sometimes stung in the night?
Will you have buried the fears that made you a prisoner in the light?
Are you at peace with your truths?
Did you amend your lies?
Can you forgive that one who still lays hidden in disguise?

When it's all said and done,
And God holds out his hands,
Can you walk into heaven?
Or will you no longer be able to stand?

Make peace with your demons.
Lay to rest your stolen past.
Fall in love without thinking.
Spend each day as if it's your last.
For we don't know, the last time you'll open your eyes,
So make the most out of today as if it's time to say goodbye.

Bridget Ford

Unstoppable

Push towards your dreams.
Bury your broken past.
It's you.
Your moment.
Your peace.
Your journey.
You have the key,
To be more than what they see.
It's your moment.
Your peace.
Fight to succeed and refuse to leave.
Don't walk away from the journey that's next.
Don't dismiss the future and ignore it as less.
Here is where you start.
Here is where you begin.
Outside of the insecurities,
Failure is what you condemn.
Embrace the test.
Work for the best.
Allow yourself to lay dead to flesh.
Push for your dreams.
Use what was given to succeed.
It's your time.
Your chance.
Your moment.
Make it last.
Be as humble as a saint but better than a champion.
Climb to the top and rest in the ambience.
Push for the chance to be *unstoppable*.

Bridget Ford

Peace is a choice.
Understand that rage, fear, and loneliness can have a negative impact on your future, your peace, and your life.
Though some utilize these emotions as the drive behind their aspirations, it can have devastating consequences if not properly addressed.
Peace comes with patience and patience comes through acceptance.
Peace is a process, but once it's achieved it's authority is as dominant as a lion, as humble as a survivor, and as soothing as a song.
Start the process.
Allow yourself to dictate your mental well-being.
You matter.
You are loved.
You deserve the chance to achieve peace.

About the Author

Bridget Ford is a hardworking mother, wife, and Registered Nurse who devotes her time to helping others through difficult situations in their lives. She obtained a Master's Degree of Science in Nursing Education despite the odds. Despite being independent, since she was seventeen, she still managed to find the light in a dark place and use it to achieve success. She continues to use that same drive and motivation to assist friends, family, students, men, and women reach their own level of peace by providing support, love, prayer, and comfort.

Black & Beautiful

Black is defined by skin tone.
Woman is defined by anatomy.
Who is the black woman through the lens of an African American?
Strong.
Courageous.
Fearless.
Are the words that echo through the tone in her voice,
The confidence in her walk,
And the grace in her step.
She conquers her fears,
Withstands the storm,
And fights for her children, her future, and her family.
From the lens of another human being, who is she?
She may be seen as aggressive,
Loud,
Uneducated,
Even with the highest degree.
Through the lens of another human being
The black woman is portrayed as the submissive.
That must be put down like a disobedient cat who refuses to adhere to the ego of its master.
Who is the black woman?
For me, she is me.
Still fighting in a world that claims to be free.

Bridget Ford

Craving More?

Stay tuned for my next book! We will uncover the struggles that minorities continue to face in the 21st Century! The battle didn't end with slavery! We are still prisoners to a world that was not framed to include pigmentation.

Two Faces

Never forget your history.
Never dismiss your past,
That breathed before your life ever touched God's hands.
We are black.
We are here.
And we are still fighting to be free.
Though the beatings aren't as frequent,
And the cries aren't as loud,
We're still cursed with the order to always bow down.
The decree to be less.
The plea that we are blessed.
Entertain the lies you'll fail the test.
You are me,
And I am you.
We both have to hide ourselves to be allowed in the room.
We are still beautiful,
Naked or clothed.
Never let too much pigment show.
Pretentiousness must be a trait you gloat when the doors are closed.
Yes, success in the black community has been maintained.
Our colleagues understand,
We will never be the same.
Maybe later but not today.
Even our names have others afraid.
The intimidation that sparks before our foot greets the floor.
The fear that leaps when pigmentation is explored.
We carry our grace in a different way.
Because even today we are not the same.
We are still black and ashamed.
Ask the second face that also carries your name.

Bridget Ford

Letter to You

You are an amazing woman. You are still strong. You are still beautiful. Those qualities and attributes will never change. Dissect the pieces that define your life, your world, and your happiness. Are you content? When you gaze into the mirror and get lost in your eyes, what do you see? How do you interpret the silent image that stands before you? I just want you to be happy. I want your smile to compete with the sun. I want your feet to fall asleep in the sand. I want your mind to be at peace. You are my mother, but a woman first. I saw you then and I see you now. You are still that woman who can demand respect by your presence. You are still that woman who can make a princess shamefully jealous. You are beautiful and what you've taught me will always be a part of me. Despite the dismay, I will always love you. I just want you to be happy. If you are unhappy, you have enough power to change it.

With Love,
Bridget

Dead While Breathing . . .

        Never forget the night your spirit drowned in your tears. It was in those nights that you questioned defeat, cried for peace, and prayed for sleep. Internal peace is often neglected. Though it's hidden, it's importance still echoes through our bodies and reflects in our appearance.

        We must incorporate the lessons we learned in each battle, won or lost. We must apply our strengths, tears, and disappointments to our future. It is mandatory that we push for what we deserve, mourn what we miss, and apply what we lost. Each test can benefit you. You just have to be willing to adjust. Adjust to the journey of sustained peace. Let your scars be a reflection of the strength that continues to uplift you each and every day.

. . . Let my Scars Tell the Story

Soul. Truth. Love. Poetry. LC

www.ingramcontent.com/pod-product-compliance
Lightning Source LLC
Chambersburg PA
CBHW070550090426
42735CB00013B/3141